First Edition, *2015*

ACKNOWLEDGEMENTS

To my friends without whose never-failing sympathy and encouragement this book would have been finished in half the time and with love for my family who are the light of my life, my rocks, and my safe place.

ABOUT THE AUTHOR

Uday veer Singh is an Indie Author, a Blogger & an activist who is born in India. He created Theory of Mankind to be used as a medium to discuss all the ideas of his mind through words and learn from others about the ideas that I can never think of. His major influences include Adolf Hitler, Jason Silva, Neil Tyson, Bill Gates, Steve Jobs and Dr.APJ Abdul Kalam.

More about his can be learned through his social networks including:

Twitter- *@beinguv*

Wikipedia- *goo.gl/7h14ah*

TABLE OF CONTENTS

WHO'S WATCHING YOU?

The Internet is flooded with numerous trackers, advertisers & unwanted beacons placed on the web by advertising & information selling companies, including Google & Facebook that are interested in your activities. And most of the time we don't even know how they collect that information, use it and even what that information consist of. But, when we look at your daily websites from a technical view, there are a lot of shadows hidden from your eyes that are watching all your activity, following your each click.

WHY COMPANIES TRACK YOUR ACTIVITY?

Of course they do it for money, they collect information about us & our interests then use that information to present some ads related to stuff we like and on the sites we visit. And there are now pop-up ads, ads with music and so on, there are many types of ads, but all have a common target to gain audience's attention; to gain YOUR attention.

Mainly, this whole process of tracking & following is used to gain information about the web user and change the Internet of ads according to it. And this analysis of visitor behavior is known as Website visitor tracking or WVT.

IS IT USEFUL OR HARMFUL?

In a way, it is useful for the economy as that analysis of the individual's web activity can be used to provide that visitor with content related to his/her preferences and it could be either during or after a visit on the site. But on the other hand, it also has an added danger of selling or theft of personal data along its usage by the spammers and hackers. And according to Internet's rules and acts of various regions, if this thing is done without the knowledge of a user, it's considered a breach of browser security.

ARE YOU READY TO TAKE AN ACTION AGAINST THEM? YOU CAN'T!

Before you make your way to the court or police station, make sure that you didn't give them permission to track or watch you. You must me thinking that why would you do that. But according to the facts, over 94% of people do that. Just think how many time does anyone of us ever read those "Terms and Conditions" before ticking the box to accept them. Who has got time for that? Isn't it Right? NO! You should take the time to read them, they are important and fun as well, sometimes. Take the example of Apple's terms & conditions, if you will read them, you will find a line saying that "You can't use Apple products to build nuclear weapons!" sounds weird? But above all, most of the terms & conditions documents that you agree to give websites proper permission to track you, follow you and also, to use Cookies. So, I would recommend you that you should always read the "Privacy Policies" rather than just lying that you have read all the terms & conditions before accepting them and surely, you will face a low crisis.

HOW DO THEY DO THAT?

This process of tracking works with something that is just like e-drones that move along your every click, keeping an eye on all your internet activity. Remember, when you just checked an item on an e-shopping site and at just next site you will see numerous ads related to that item? This works according to due to their strategy to make you see the things again and again, and convince you to buy them. Even most of the Internet users feel anonymity while browsing, yet their extensive personal information is getting collected within seconds of your opening a site.

And if we read the Google's privacy policy then we will find that this information consists of a lot of private data including telephony log information, device-specific information, cookies, name, email address, telephone number or credit card etc.

Actually, it all depends on a single term: **The Cookies!** You may have heard of this term in a lot of web articles and also, from your Mom's mouth. (But these cookies don't taste as good as your mother's cookies.) Web Cookies are the text bits that your browser downloads as you surf the web. And these carry some useful information about your interaction with the web. So, if you visit a website that you have visited before, your browser and the website as well, will know that you have been there before. And if you use a different computer, open a new web browser or delete your cookies, that website will treat you as this is your first visit. Cookies actually help in faster and improved functioning of browser and in a way the web tries to learn your preferences. Like the YouTube remembers the volume of the video player that you used last time and automatically adjusts it. Just the same way Facebook try to understand their users and put the top stories according to your interests in your newsfeed. And summing up, with these small things Cookies help to make the user experience better. And same does your mommy's cookies to your stomach. But the question that arises here is that:

I will not say that you have to worry too much, but you sometimes you have to be careful about them. So, exactly what can you do about that? Blocking any kind of trackers on the Internet is very easy with the help of some easy to use some software Ghostery, Disconnect or Lightbeam that have an ability to cull over 1,900 trackers and 2,300 tracking patterns. And in a way you just need to keep your cookies safe and browse in a more private & secure way, here are some tips about how you do that:

- **Eat them in a private place:** You can do your daily searches in incognito mode or surf the whole web in an Anonymous mode. I mean, just do the work that needs privacy in a private manner. And if you want to do it in a simple way, just go incognito mode. (Using chrome? Press Ctrl+ Shift+ N)
- **Keep your cookies in a Jar:** You can use a Privacy Protection Software or a simple browser extension to block all the trackers. Also, simple things like deleting your cookies at a regular interval and use the private mode whenever you can do help you protect them.

- **Cookies are not for Sharing:** Seriously, just like the passwords, don't let anyone steal your cookies. You never know what that person can use that information for, from cracking your passwords to hacking your private life. And in the following chapters you will learn how you can do it without compromising your browsing experience & time.

GOLDEN RULES OF WEB BROWSING!

Remember? Whenever you buy a new product you get a manual that along its uses, teaches you about the precautions you have to make while using that product. But we miss these precautions while using the Internet, so this chapter is all about those precautions. You will learn what they are, should we worry about them, and how what harms can take place it not taken seriously. So, let's start from a simple topic-

THE FAKE ACCOUNTS:

By definition, they are those social-networking accounts that someone creates using someone else's name and information. This could be a celebrity's duplicate account or something just created to harass someone. In short, we can call them "a virtual con artist". And according to the stats, More than 9% of Facebook accounts are detected fake, but the amount of undetected fake accounts is way higher. Also, up to 97% of them are of females. Studies also reveal that in their "real" accounts, people only fill about 35% of their genuine information, which raise the question that

DO YOU NEED TO WORRY ABOUT THEM?

With every following day, websites like Facebook are on the way of becoming safer so that the level of spam and malicious links can also be minimized. Along that the advertising companies on the social networks want to be sure that they receive a more genuine audience, not the fake guys as increasing proportion of these dodgy accounts is one big problem for the advertisers. Other than them they also affect the normal users as these accounts are used by people to fool others and gain some personal profit along spreading spam across the network. So, you do need to do something about them, but before that we need to differentiate between a fake & real account.

HOW CAN WE DETECT ONE?

There's no perfect way to find one, but following the quick tutorial below will surely help you guessing better:

- **Check their Photos:** If an account contains only one or even no photos of the individual then there are good chances that the account is a fake one. Try Googling some random profile pics, most commonly, account makers often get theirs from a random Google search.
- **Their recent activities:** If that user was just been adding random people, making new friends, liking random pages, joining random groups, it suggests that the profile is fake and the person is just there for time passing and getting anonymously popular.
- **"Show me your friends and I will tell your fortune":** If that person has added or followed many people of the opposite gender, this suggests that the account is made for fun or random dating.
- **Check the basic Info:** Check if there is any ideal school, workplace or birthplace and if the person's information feels fake it could be a fake one. And

many of the fake accounts have unique birth dates like 1 Jan, **** or 31 Dec, ****. Also, do check the links they've provided to personal websites, social media pages, etc.

Now that you can detect one, you must be wondering how you can immune yourself from one, but before moving to that point you should about a similar security threat known as Phishing.

WHAT ACTUALLY IS PHISHING?

A phishing website, email or message work in a way that it tricks you to reveal your personal information such as bank account, contact details and mostly your passwords. It's the most popular type of hacking and also, the easiest one according to the hackers like me. But more important thing is that we should think that "Why hackers consider this easiest?" The answer is that most of us are simply not aware. For example, most of us as soon as they see an appealing offer tend to click it without even thinking that if that offer can even be possible.

The real reason behind phishing depends eventually on the hacker's intention. Mainly, they will try to attain the following details:

- Username or password
- Bank account number, security details or full credit card numbers
- Your mother's maiden name (In case, it's your security question's answer.)

- And your personal details like your family details school or email etc.

And for the purpose they will use Emails, tweets, online advertisement and anything that you can click on. When you click on what they want you to click, you get smartly redirected to fake sign-in screens, where they simply try to steal your passwords. If you want to know what their success depends on, it just depends on our foolishness and carelessness. As I said above, we just don't think before clicking!

WHAT ARE THE GOLDEN RULES TO PROTECT YOU FROM THEM?

- **Don't talk to strangers:** This is a common but ignored tip. You should think twice before accepting friend requests from the stranger and if you want to be sure that you are safe then you can ask a few questions to them like How did they find out about you?; Who do you know in common?; Why they added you? Or just who they are?
- **Be a detective:** Use the tips that you read before and detect if the person that tried to contact you is real.
- **Limit connections:** Change your connection settings so that people with a mutual connection with you or your friends can contact you. Doing this is very simple in any social network; just go to Settings then privacy. Also, you can block them if needed. For the Facebookers, you can easily block

friend requests or even the person if you don't have a good feeling about him/her. You can also block them from bothering you and even report Facebook if you feel that they are harmful to you.

- **Turn on the eagle vision:** Here, I mean that before clicking on any website that you are not familiar with, check its URL first. Mostly, they are designed to look like a real company's website or email, but they just can't simply cover the whole thing as most of the domain selling website make sure that the URL is used for a business or personal purpose, rather than something illegal like hacking.

  E.g.: Facebook's real web address is *"https://www.Facebook.com"*, but if a hacker sent it to you, it will be something like *"http://xyz.facebook.com"* so, it's simple to detect one. And when the beginners do this, their URL is even easier to detect as they will use something like: *"http://freehostingsite.xyz.com/facebook.php"*.

- **Use a smart browser:** Web browsers like Chrome or Firefox have the ability to auto-detect a phishing website and give you a warning before you visit that website. And for this purpose you just need to make sure that your browser is smart enough to detect the hack.

- **Don't trust everyone:** You simply don't need to open every email attachment or click every link that you receive by any unknown person. Before taking any action make sure that legitimate, you can simply check the email address or the person's profile and if it doesn't feel safe to you, just simply delete it or save others by marking it as a scam.

- When you receive an email with a tagline "Congratulation you have won an iPhone" or something like "A person has left you his property while dying" or "Hi, I am XYZ and I want to be your friend", these types of emails or messages are scams in almost every case. (Some people can be truly lucky to get something like that in real.) So, just don't do what they say and use the above Guidelines to protect yourself.

Following these simple rules and increasing your attention span will surely help you to get rid of those spammers or phishers, but what else can you do to increase your security level? You will learn many smart ways in the following chapters.

IMMUNE
WEB

I.

FIRST LEARN
THE RULES

THEN BREAK THEM

II.

UDAY VEER SINGH

2015-2016

THUGS OF THE INTERNET

As some of you may have already guessed, in this chapter we will learn about the Cyber-Bullies who use the internet to harass & even blackmail people. So, let's begin by answering the basic question that:

WHAT IS CYBER-BULLYING?

Cyber-Bullying is the verbal, emotional or mental abuse to anyone through the Internet. Facebook, YouTube, Twitter, and Skype are the fun & useful sites that we use every day, but they are also the base of the Cyber-bullying and most of the victims are students. It's a kind of Virtual weapon that people use to harm others digitally.

The reason behind its increasing number of cases isn't that the number of bullies is huge or the victims don't have the power, but it's growing because people don't complain; they just don't want to fight back! According to a research, Only 1 in 10 victims will report this crime to their parents or any other adult which are the reason they don't get their problems solved and unfortunately, the victims are 2 to 9 times more likely to commit suicide rather than fighting back. Also, as over 80% of teens worldwide use their cell phone at a regular interval, Mobile is the most common medium of bullying. And if you are wondering about its disastrous effects, here are the facts:

- About 43% of the kids have been bullied online and there are more girls in the "victim" list of Cyber-Bullying than boys; almost twice than boys.
- Feel that the world has understood Love? Think again; every 9 out of 10 LGBTQ teens experience harassment online.
- It kills! CB is the most common reason for suicide cases in youth.
- And those cases which don't end in death, these ends leaving the long-term or even permanent damage to the victims' mind.
- Afraid to go to school as you may be bullied? The number of "cyberbullied" victims is greater than any other type of bullied victims.

WHO ARE THESE BULLIES?

He/ she can be anyone who has the access to the internet along the thoughts to hurt someone. There is no specific kind or type of bullies, but they can be anyone who hates you or is jealous of you. In some cases, even the teachers & relatives are behind this crime. And the number bullies are more on the Internet than real life bullies who can use anyway to irritate you. And above all, bullying really sucks!

But, there must be a reason behind their actions; actually, there is more than reason that we can think of:

- **Jealousy:** This the most common reason behind Bullying. People think that you are better than them and when they can't become as good, they try to bring you down, this is in human's blood, so they just do it!

- **False beliefs:** Some of them believe that they are powerful, some think that others deserve that treatment. This often revolves around a person's social or economic status and the society develops a stereotype thinking for some people which later turn out to become a BIG cause of bullying.
- **Revenge:** There is always someone who will feel unjustified by your actions and the reason for this can be tormenting from the past. And through cyber-bullying, they get a sense of relief and vindication for what they have experienced.
- **Entertainment:** This may sound weird, but many people actually practice cyberbullying just as a source of entertainment because they just want to add some excitement and drama to their lives.
- **Symbol of Power:** Many people do relate Cyber Bullying to power; they think that people who practice this are more powerful than others. They also think this as a great social status and use Internet to express aggression and that mean girl behavior.

There can be numerous more reasons behind it, but it's more important how you treat this whole thing that finding the reason behind it. Before moving to the tackling Cyber-bullying part, let's try to answer this question first.

DO YOU THINK THAT BULLIES DESERVE A CHANCE TO IMPROVE?

Actually, the answer to this question was quite controversial & somewhat complicated so, I decided to ask my audience through a poll and here's what I got:

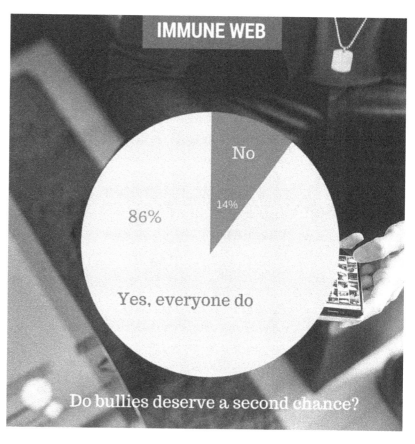

86% (That's a big number) of people think that just like everybody, bullies also deserve a chance to improve. But when we look at the rest **14%,** this represents the people who are somehow related to or involved in Bullying and think that every bully deserves punishment. Being a writer, I am still confused on choosing any side; one represents the moral thinking while other expresses the grief & feeling of revenge. So for the final conclusion, let us look at it from both viewpoints.

People who were somehow involved in the process of Bullying think that this process should be ended as soon as possible!

Those who choose, what I call, the fighter's side, think that as every real-life criminal is punished as per their level of crime the cyber criminals should also be treated similarly no discrimination or self-profit should be there. I do agree on this. But every criminal in the same crime isn't equal, in some cases, the words of M.K. Gandhi prove to be right, he says that "Forgiveness is the attribute of the strong."

And everyone should be given a proper chance of self-improvement. We should give at least one chance to the bullies so that they can recreate their image; some of them can improve! I personally know a lot of people who wanted to improve & did it perfectly; they worked and created a brand new & better image of themselves in the society.

So, after thinking about the situation from alternate sides, we can see that somehow both sides just want the "END" of Cyber-bullying. We all just want this crappy practice to stop and for the criminals, they can either be given a chance to improve or should be punished on the basis of the activity. Even though, most the world's Governments doesn't have any powerful laws or rights against cyber crimes like Cyber-Bullying, there are still many active groups that are using the same internet to fight them.

But you can't rely on anyone else for your own protection, so here's the things you can do to immune yourself.

SO, WHAT SHOULD YOU DO WHEN TARGETED BY THE THUGS?

- **Ignoring them-** This is the most effective & powerful way to fight them, just like the real life, ignore them in the Virtual world too. You can block them, unfollow them or just simply don't look. Of course, doing this is not easy as it sounds but until you stopped paying attention this will keep hurting you; they don't deserve your attention!
- **Get the Help-** Tell your parents, friends, relatives or anyone you trust but stop hiding this. If u kept it to yourself it will never end, you cannot make this journey alone; you have to report it. You have the rights to report.
- **Just STOP it-** As I said earlier, it sucks; it really sucks! So just get up & give him what he deserve, don't think about the result, just end this and if you were right you will not lose. Raise your voice; turn up the volume and let the devil out!
- **Be active:** All the tips above were for the people who are victims of bullying, but this one is the Bystanders who see the whole thing but never react. These are the people who see the aggressive or insulting post about someone but never report it; just scroll down. So, just take action and stand for the right and make the Criminal Pay. The movement when the Bystanders start taking a decision; the movement they raise voice is the time when the change will come!

And after all these tips for the victims & the bystanders, here's a single advice that the bullies need:

"To have once been a criminal is no disgrace. To remain a criminal is the disgrace." — *Malcolm X*

This was all that you need to learn about the subject of cyber-bullying, but if you want to feel or explore what it feels to be its victim, the next chapter will help you in the task. And before folding this page, just keep in mind to stand up for yourself as well as others and report or fight the Bully rather than standing idly.

" THE WORST KIND OF CRIME IS IGNORING THE CRIME. "

UDAY VEER SINGH

IS AN INDIAN AUTHOR OF A NUMBER OF BLOGS & BOOKS ON HUMANITY, INTERNET & PHILOSPHY

A STORY WITH 3 ENDINGS

I am sure you have heard this quote before; if not then this story will perfectly make you understand what does it stands for. This story is of a young & beautiful soul who used to the internet to make her way to the world. Along the meaning of this quote, this story will also help you feel what you have read about in the last chapter. So, here it is.

Her name was **Jasmine,** she was one on the finest looking girls from her school along with a very sharp mind like God has made her with full dignity; a beauty with a brain! Almost everyone who knows her personally loved her personality and along with all this, she was also a wonderful writer, she loved to write about the world; about the places she had traveled; about great people she had met and so on.

But she didn't want to keep those stories; those views to herself, she was looking for a platform where she can tell the whole world that what she really was and to show the real power of her pen. In her search for a platform, she got a really exciting tool, everyone was crazy about it and it was also a great source of information collecting, it was the "Internet"! One of her friends introduced her to this virtual world, she was really excited to share her words and she did so. Even, it was at a small scale, but she gained a lot of readers and with every coming day she kept on unfolding the Internet of things, and finally she met her new friend the "Social Network"; the giant place where everyone had something to share and talk about.

She then started sharing her words at this place, but she was unaware of that this place is full of people who will not only judge her views but her life. As soon as she started sharing her ideas here, some people raised their hands to support her, but the hands to pull her down were in a much greater number. One of her most popular articles on the social network was about the Inner beauty that every person had; it gained a lot of audiences although they were interested in her, more than her article. Just after publishing it, she started receiving the messages and comments of the people:

These types of messages didn't stop and when she tried to

Jasmine
"Beauty is not in the face; beauty is a light in the heart!"
missing. Hey, my this weekend's article is about the Inner Beauty You will be albe to read soon.

Like · Comment · Share

👍 12 people likes this.

 Robin Come to me, I will show you how to make love! <3 ;) :p
10 minutes ago · Like

 Andrew CHeCk yoUr iNbOx WHy dOn'T yOu rePly biTcH!!!
9 minutes ago · Like

 Tommy Send me your NUMBER plzzzzz!!!
9 minutes ago · Like · 👍 1

 Sam u r more beautiful than your article... first show me your complete outer beauty than we will talk about the inner one.
7 minutes ago · Like

💬 View more comments

Write a comment...

take the help of her friends, they completely ignored her saying this is all normal. She tried her best to get herself out of this but failed. She was afraid to tell her parents or teachers as they don't want her stay within a limited border; within a boundary or rules, guidelines and not to dos. With every day, these comments & messages became cheaper and all that she could do was nothing. Finally, she made a decision to quit the Internet, but somehow one of those managed to get her number and started teasing her with the prank, blank or abusive calls.

Now, she was even afraid to walk alone in the street as those negative words followed her everywhere in her mind she always felt like someone is watching her and is ready to judge. But like every human she had a limit, her friend, who introduced her to the world of the Internet was the one who found her body, covered utterly with blood in the school's toilet.

Oh Yes! She managed to get rid of those voices; those judgments that she was afraid of. A word player who became afraid of the words left everyone wordless.

So, did you enjoy the story because I didn't! Again a woman was pushed out of the race of life with by negativity; by the judgment system; by the social network! But what if the story didn't go this way? What if this story can be an inspiration for us? Let's re-imagine the story from the time she starting receiving those negative comments.

It was the time when everyone was against her, every comment that she got was making her closer to the end, but this time a light of hope came:

Michael
Hey, Jasmine! I found that some guys are crossing their limits.

I'm here to help in any way if you need!

Jasmine
I was so tensed after receiving those negative comments and messages, but your words gave me some satisfaction. And I will be so grateful if you taught me how can I get rid of them.

Michael
This Social Network also has features to help you block or report these guys. Follow me and I will tell you some of the very useful security tools of the site.

Jasmine
Thank you so much!!!
Tell me what to do!

Michael, one of her close friend, made her aware of every aspect that helped her to tackle any negativity on this anti-social-network he also unfolded some other important points to her feel more free to express her ideas.

In this way, he became the prince who rescued her princess from the dragon of social judgment.

But why do the stereotypes always says that the price saved the princess? And why does our story even need to follow them? Let's try to change it one last time.

This time, the story goes on like this, being a writer, Jasmine had also written about the working and dealing of the negativity. She knew how to make these guys shut up, she didn't need to block or report them, also she don't want someone to help her dealing with it; she had the ability to fight them in her own way. She was brave enough to stay strong and smart enough to teach them a lesson. Here is how she dealt with the situation:

Jasmine
"Beauty is not in the face; beauty is a light in the heart!" missing. Hey, my this weekend's article is about the Inner Beauty You will be albe to read soon.

Like · Comment · Share

👍 12 people likes this.

Robin Come to me, I will show you how to make love! <3 ;) :p
10 minutes ago · Like

Andrew CHeCk yoUr iNbOx WHy dOn'T yOu rePly biTcH!!!
9 minutes ago · Like

Tommy Send me your NUMBER plzzzzz!!!
9 minutes ago · Like · 👍 1

Sam u r more beautiful than your article... first show me your complete outer beauty than we will talk about the inner one.

Jasmine Hello! Thanks everyone for sharing their viewpoints here. Also, thank you for telling that some of you are not even a man as a true man is the one who understands and respects a woman's feelings. Most people think that social media is a platform to say anything without having any repercussions.
10 minutes ago · Like

And with that Clerk, she fought like a super(Wo)man

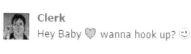

Clerk
Hey Baby 🤍 wanna hook up? 😊

Jasmine
What? Who are You?

Clerk
Don't be rude lady! i will treat you better than a bitch

Jasmine
Please shut up!

Clerk
Come on! Okay just give my your number!!

🤍 🤍 🤍 🤍 🤍 🤍 🤍 🤍 😄

Clerk
:0

Clerk
RePly!!!

Clerk
🤍 Dn't B shy

Jasmine
Hey, You are a true inspiration to all the jerks out there. You are
doing a great work in creating a big shame for male fraternity.
The movement you sent me the message I realized that you can't
even respect any woman, including your mother, sister or anyone.
And you wanted to hangout with me? I am so sorry as being a
human, humanity doesn't allows me to date who has lost his
ability to give respect.

Her actions defined the real power; the real beauty of the
woman that have the power to save any prince from any
powerful beast.

Now, I feel satisfied with the story so, if you have read this thoroughly, we will now learn about the factors that affected and modeled the alternate endings of the story:

- **Independence**: As you saw, if Jasmine had proper knowledge and confidence then no man or woman would dare to do anything against her. She can be independent and self-sufficient; only if she gets proper knowledge.
- **Help:** Even if you lack knowledge, you should surround yourself with people like Michael who will support you in any problem just like a true friend, unlike Jasmine's other friends who ignored her problems and just moved on.
- **Awareness:** Imagine the internet where everyone has proper knowledge and confidence to tackle any attacks or problems, after that there will be no one daring to post negative comments or send abusive messages.
- **Responsibility:** Think if the social sites get more active; they get a technology update through which every spam message or post gets removed before even you see it. Also, these sites can help people to learn about the cyber security and web working.

So, before we end, there are some things that I want to tell you that this whole story inspired by thousands of stories that I researched while writing this, including the some stories from the people very close to me. I hope you got something that you can use personally from the Jasmine's life. But what if Jasmine's ID was instead targeted by the hackers who tried to steal her password? How can she get an unbreakable code to protect her virtual kingdom? The next chapter is all about making that perfect code.

WHAT MAKES A PASSWORD PERFECT?

The process of making this perfect code and protect your virtual treasure can be a tricky work and a long one too. So, we have divided this whole thing into three different sections for making it easier to understand and work on.

MAKING THE PASSWORD

- Use 12 characters or more.
- A mixture of Uppercase (ABCD) & lowercase (abcd) alphabets along at least two or three numbers (123).
- You can have punctuation or symbols to make it safer. (,:;-!? or @&+=>$#*)
- Turn phrases into codes (I am the dumbest creature-IATDC), it's safe & easy to remember.
- You may use some non-English characters as 96% of the hackers just have an English keyboard.

KEEPING IT SAFE!

TO DO:

- Write it down, in case you forget that, but make sure you keep it in a very SAFE place.
- Change it several times during a year, but not too often, 2 times will work. (Passwords are like underwears, change them often.)
- Use powerful Antivirus software that will protect you from Trojan horses, key loggers, and other malicious hacking tricks.

NOT TO DO:

- Do avoid obviously or easy passwords like "12345", "ABCD" or "password".
- Try not to use biographical information like the school or college name, company, pet or birthday
- Avoid common or simple dictionary words
- Do not tell your password to anyone. (At any condition!)
- Don't reuse or recycle your old passwords.
- Try not use just one single password for all of your accounts at least have a small difference. (You will learn how at the next page.)

REMEMBERING THE PASSWORD:

- Keep a backup, maybe you can forget it.
- Use a password manager, easiest way to remember and feel safe.

- Personalize it with each site, it will be different for each site; safe & easy to remember; personal touch. E.G.:
  - FB1234Abcd$ (FB- Facebook)
  - TT1234Abcd$ (TT- Twitter)
  - IG1234Abcd$ (IG- Instagram)

Now, if you follow all these steps I am sure not one from a computer geek like me to a professional hacker can crack your security code unless, the point a gun at your head and make you type it. Anyways, this can be true for just a one in a million case.

HOW WE LITERALLY KILL OTHERS ON THE INTERNET!

"I never met her in real life, we just talked on the web.

But I am sure that she was a really beautiful. She loved sharing "what's on her mind" but, unfortunately, the world she loved didn't like her that much.

She got disgrace, haterade & jealousy in return of her feelings. And as the last option she chooses to quit this judging world and I never heard anything from her again."

What harms can your words make? It was just a small comment, right? No!

It was bigger and due to our comments; due to us, many beautiful souls die and another gets up to have their place until someone again judges, what's on their mind.

So, as you have read about in some previous pages describing the current situation of this so-called "Developed" world. We judge others by their actions, but ourselves by our intentions. And everyone from the person who just scroll down to the one who likes or support one of those negative comments become a part of it; part of the crime, that hurts a person's mind. It's the mother which gives birth to that child which we call CyberBullying. Yes! It's a part of it and most the time it develops a base for the bullies to attack the victims.

"IGNORING FACTS DOES NOT MAKE THEM GO AWAY."

Earlier, we talked a lot about how we can fight cyber-bullying, but there are some ways that will just cost our common sense and will help to kill it before its birth. Also, these will ensure that you don't help in the growth of this crime.

- **Report, Block or Ask:** You already know how you can report anything on Facebook, Twitter or G+, but do you use that feature? From now whenever you see a crappy comment on your or even someone else's post report it! You can even block that person or contact him or website's owner to take action about it!
- **Support the Victim:** If you know that someone is attacking your friend, you have to help your friend! It can be as simple as a back-fire comment or as powerful as a full debate; you just need to raise first (don't worry rescue will be there soon).
- **Ignore:** When you know that those people doesn't matter to you then why react? Just keep on ignoring and they will stop when they will fail to gain attention.
- **Don't Ignore:** The title may sound Ironical if compared to the above one, but you should know what the limits are and what you should do when someone cross them!
- **Watch your words:** See what you are posting; it should not be offensive to someone (if you want don't want to do it intentionally). And if your post

isn't offensive, but then someone is acting wrong then re-read the steps mentioned above.

And if we didn't do anything about our attitude towards this, this may turn Internet into a nightmare for someone. This may sound weird, but there are some people who believe that the Internet is not a safe place for everyone and some are even afraid of it. Before starting this book, I met some of these people to collect their fears and here they are, each with a personalized solution for the problem:

ARE YOU AFRAID OF THE INTERNET?

- **Dhruv Setia, Student:**

  The Internet has all my personal information; it knows everything about me. That scares me!

Yes, the internet knows a lot about you, but if you think again it only knows what you have told it. I mean, it only has the information that you have shared with the Internet. So, I will recommend you to look again about what you have shared on it and remove what you don't want to be public. And the Internet has a lot of options to protect your privacy.

- **Ravi Sharma, Trader:**

  The Internet has all my Money; it has full control over my economy. I am afraid that I can lose it!

Anyone with a lot of digital money lives in the fear of losing it due to technical problems. But these kinds of situations are very rare. And for the thieves, if we pay a little more attention at the things going around on the web, we will tackle any spam or hack leading to any kind of loss. So, just open up your Mind!

- **Anonymous:**

  The People there are fake and I just can't trust anyone.

Fake accounts are way too common nowadays, but still not everyone is fake. And on the trusting point, it's your choice to trust whomever you want, but I will recommend that you should make sure that person is at least a real one and is also someone that can't cause any harm to you.

- **Muskaan Goyal, Student:**

  I feel trapped in it! There are so many people to judge me, but why? I just can't express myself.

I know that feel, everyone you know and even people you don't know wants to comment on your opinion and the negativity there is way more than the positivity. But still you have the options to block, report or simply ignore them. And the three chapters of this book are all about dealing with this problem.

- **Alexander Thoryk:**

  Definitely the Internet isn't a safe place. Any personal information that you type on your keyboard or store on your device (PC, tablet, or Smartphone) could be stolen if that device is connected to the Internet. The Connection is two-way path: if you are connected to the Internet, the Internet is connected to you

Internet was made for connection and it has done that work too, but as the Internet was invented by the people and it's is being destroyed by the people. Actually, it's not the internet from which we fear, but it's the people of the internet who make us afraid. The only solution for this is teaching & learning about its safer usage.

A bunch of creativity arranged pixels on a screen can't possibly scare anyone unless, it's a horror movie. And it is a tool for us to connect with the world, there are no borders between people and it's also an everlasting library of knowledge, we just have to look in the right place because they have pumped this place full of propaganda. This endless library of Knowledge can be only doomed by the harmful and immoral uses of it.

So, coming to the conclusion of this chapter cum message, just imagine that you are driving a car and you suddenly see someone laying half dead on the road, will you stop or pass by? Now, think that car is your mouse; that road is your social site and that person is the victim of cyber-crime and you can easily scroll down or use your keyboard to spread some positivity and save a life! Just keep in mind that we all are responsible for every act of crime that we didn't try to stop and start standing up when you can.

WHICH IS THE BEST ANTIVIRUS OR WEB PROTECTOR? DO YOU EVEN NEED ONE?

In today's world, we all try to find a safe place to live, love & share. And when more than half of our world is digital then we always wish & try to make it safer first. For that purpose, we get the most costly Antivirus or Malware software that sometimes costs more than the device itself. So, which is the best software for your protection? And is it really important to have one? In this chapter, you will find the real need of antivirus along with some better & cheaper alternatives.

WHY DO YOU NEED AN ANTIVIRUS?

Worms, Trojan horses, viruses along the other invaders attacks our devices and for the protection from them Antivirus programs are made. Sometimes, those harmful attackers can make your computer really "Sick" along with deleting your personal & important data. So, it looks like we need an Antivirus as a bodyguard for our System.

And coming to the service time, an antivirus mainly lasts up to 1 year when you have paid for its typical subscription. And after that you have to renew the antivirus after that time period, which changes with the companies along using your valuable internet data on its security updates which are necessary to maintain the software (according to its developers).

WHY WE DON'T NEED AN ANTIVIRUS?

Most people will agree that you need an Antivirus for keeping your Devices secure, but there is a condition for it- you need a different software for every other device; computer, mobile or tablet also, they don't guarantee full protection and some even don't meet the stuff the guaranteed. According to me, it's not a kind of thing that we really need to worry about or to spend money on; there are many alternative ways that are cheaper than a typical security program. Although, you can depend on them for they do the best they can if bought from a trusted producer, but you need to know what you can do without them.

WHAT ARE THE ALTERNATIVES?

Here are some tips that will definitely work and the only thing you need to have for using them is your Brain along some common sense in it:

- **Use passwords:** The most obvious & easy thing is to have a password that no one can break and use it to secure your data. And your antivirus can't keep someone from accessing your social account or Wi-Fi; only a password can!
- **Fire up the PC:** I don't mean to burn your PC, but I am asking you to turn up the firewall which is present in

most of the Operating Systems by default; you just need to make sure it's turned on.

- **Avoid public access:** Going to the public internet cafes is not at all safe even if they give a great internet speed. When you are using a public PC, there is an added risk of losing your private Information along confidential data. Also, you have to depend on third party for your security & privacy; you can't have your antivirus everywhere.

- **Digital scams; attachments & downloads**: Ever saw that spam folder you don't care about, check it someday and you will find a bunch of big & powerful promises and funny jokes that are actually jokes on you. That all kind of stuff is considered as Spam as it can harm your PC along stealing your data. So whenever you get an email from an unknown or untrusted person always make sure that it's not a hidden malware. For this purpose, you may rely on an antivirus.

- **Save your mobile:** Nowadays, mobiles are the easiest & popular targets for the hackers, so make sure that you always lock your phone and avoid storing your sensitive personal data on the device. And use the tip mentioned above for avoiding attackers from the emails that you receive in your cell phone. If you're engaged in mobile banking then you must have some backup security other than your bank's protection, for which there are many security apps, both free & paid out there.

- **Wipe up the dust:** Use file scrubbers to wipe the temporary, unused or waste stuff from the PC & phone that take up a lot of space and sometimes come up as a virus. So, make sure that you keep your Recycle bin empty and clean the junk manually or using specified software.

Other then antivirus you use, your security also depends on the web browser you use. The question arise here is that

CAN YOUR BROWSER PROTECT YOU FROM THE HACKERS?

Earlier this year, in the "Pwn2Own hacking challenge" security researchers were challenged to hack in major browsers and unfortunately, they were able to get all major web browsers, taking home the cash prize of $240,000. It was the second day of the event when Mozilla Firefox, Microsoft Internet Explorer, Google Chrome and Apple Safari got exploited by the researchers. And the impressing thing was that one of them just took a little less than 1 second to exploit Firefox's out-of-bounds memory vulnerability. Another researcher demonstrated three different browser exploits against IE 11, Chrome and Safari.

This whole story seems to be shocking and does put a big question mark on the face of the internet security. However, we should remember that these people were some of the best security workers from around the globe, so I would recommend you not to worry much. But if you are still worried, just follow the tips you got above and stay relaxed.

But is there a real browser that can protect you from everything? Actually, yes and you will learn about this in the upcoming chapter which will explore the secrets within the world of the internet and is probably the most interesting one too.

Before ending this chapter, you should take a look at my personally favorite tool that I use not only for the web security, but also to block some websites that can be damaging for the kids like the erotica websites. As the Internet is full of dangerous & adult content, it can cause bad effects on you or your family members. So this tool that help you and I use it on my personal computer too. It's "Blue Coat's K9 Web Protection", the free & very powerful software against adult content and malware present on the Internet. In addition, this also gives the monitoring option & manual blocking option that can be protected by your personal password. Its features include:

- It's a free Internet filter and blocker for personal use.
- It protects you from scams, temptations & malware.
- It enables us to Force Safe Search on all major search engines.
- Set time restrictions to block web access.
- Monitor and control web activity.
- It has more than 70 categories, including gambling, drugs, racism, spyware and phishing.
- Automatic content ratings: real-time site analysis.

WOMEN AND THE INTERNET

"You educate a man; you educate a man. You educate a woman; you educate a family." — *Brigham Young*

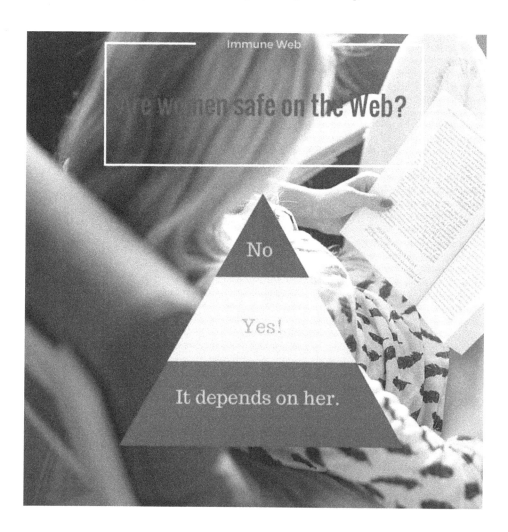

DO YOU THINK WOMEN ARE SAFE ON THE INTERNET?

This question often bothers me and to reach the best answer I thought to ask it to my audience, most women. Here's what I unfolded through it.

As you can see through the graph on the first page of this chapter, 26% of the total audience believes that this virtual world is safe for the ladies and only 10% people think that this world is not at all safe for women. And more interestingly the majority; 64% believe that it all depends on the woman and her actions that she performs on the web. We will discuss various factors affecting this below.

WHAT'S THE CAUSE?

The problem isn't only that women are more likely to be treated badly on the web, but also that most of them don't take any action against it. According to several research & surveys, as women are more targeted in cyber crimes and due to this many ladies just don't use the internet as they are afraid of it. If we have a look at the tech industry, we will find that we're missing out on the innovations and creations that the ladies around the globe can make. So, the problem is not only the ways of treatment, but also the ways in which we react to it. If more women are tech geeks or at least have some good basics of its working they can make this place safer, not only for themselves, but for everyone else too.

And thinking about the factors that affect this whole thing, we can come up to the following items:

- **There are many pervs on the web:** This was actually one of the comments that I got on the poll and the internet is really full of people that just use it for teasing others & the motive can be something serious or something crappy as flirting. But seriously this needs to be stopped!
- **Ladies don't fight back:** Every time a woman receives a spam message from anyone she has a choice to ignore or make him realize his place, but unfortunately 4 out of every 5 women choose to just ignore the person. I believe that if they at least try to fight back, the situation can be a lot better.
- **Lack of knowledge**: If we talk about a particular country then there are more tech geek women than men in US who have that great knowledge that I can't imagine having, but looking from the global view there is a scarcity of women who are interested in the scene behind the working web. Many women use the web, but as compared the men only a few of them try to learn about the working of the internet or its security. This is just, Sad.
- **Lack of resources:** The number of encouragements, the number of teachers and the number of resources to make people learn about the web is still very low. Even if we inspect the schools, their computer classes teach kids how to use Excel, word or sometimes one paragraph of antivirus. But the number of resources that can actually show us the real face of the internet and how it is affecting our life is very less. Due to this not only women, but everyone is highly affected.
- **The stereotype thinking:** We keep on thinking that men are responsible for the safety of the women but

in real the women are. I think that women don't need these so called "strong" men for them, they can become independent if we stop treating them as inferior, even this chapter's title feels like that, but it is important as a wake-up call for them, whose motto is to make them realize the issues, their causes and of course the solutions.

"We do not need to attend classroom training programs for everything. Observation opens the windows of knowledge around us."

LET'S TALK ABOUT THE SOLUTIONS:

- **Lend a helping hand:** There are numerous computer bloggers and geeks like me here and if we all worked to teach others what we know we can easily able to bring a change. Its start could be small, but it will gain power as it will spread by person to person like a viral disease; disease to be safe and make others safe too. (Yes. we are the Change!)
- **World cheat the fools only:** One of my readers said that web is not safe for idiots or people who can't handle themselves. She meant that internet is just like the real world economy; the game of the name. If we learnt about the psychology of this virtual world along with its working, we can easily fight back most of the convicts present out there.
- **Sharing is Saving:** Girls keep on sharing all the stuff with their gossip gals so, why not some techy girls or even boys share these things with their best buddies so that they can make their circles safe on the web.

- **Using internet for the internet:** What can't we learn from the web? We can also use it for its own safety; you just need to Google it right.
- **Share & Solve:** If we kept our problems hidden deep inside us then there will be no solution to them. You can share your problems with anyone you trust; it can be your friends, family members or anyone. Even I get regular mails & calls from the people who need my help and if someone shares his/her problem with you, you can use your skills to solve their problem and together make the world safe. (Only if you know how)

Once we have ensured everyone's safety it is important that we end their fear too. As I wrote in the previous chapters some people doesn't use internet just because they are afraid of it, but if we want we can make them realize it is not something to fear, rather it is more useful than your Math teacher. There are many organizations like Google working to get the women, also men on the internet. We can too, teach our known ones to try the internet of things for anything they want, from cooking recipes to husband repairing, but surely in a safer way.

WHAT DO WOMEN THINK OF THE WEB?

Katriel Patience: *I strongly believe that the internet is safe for women for a lot of reasons. The two simple reasons are, we can multitask and we apply what we learn from motherhood to office work.*

Katriel sounds like a powerful person to me. But still there are a lot of people who are unaware of the vices of the virtual web and get harmed by it regularly. And in the process of development we have to work along the known, as well as unknown; we simply can't leave anyone behind.

Dustin Bennett: *Her safety depends on that if the woman wants attention and doesn't get what she thought well that's her fault if it's someone who was hacked they should be protected by all.*

If we give everyone proper education about the Internet and its safety then there will no need to worry about anything. She will do whatever she wants to do and in her own style, undisturbed.

Monsieur Africain: *I personally believe that women need to become more involved in tech and engineering. That isn't to say that women aren't becoming involved in it, but the number is relatively low. Not everyone is an engineer, though. Both men and women can be phished, hacked, and the sort. There are men also that need plenty of help in the virtual community as well. Not just women.*

I completely agree with these views and I wish that too. Also, we can't forget that women are the most popular target thus forcing us to work for them first! But surely, if the improvement process went smoothly along the support of people like Monsieur, the beam of hope is a big one.

Contracts IT: *Interesting, although it's one that does depend highly on other factors such as the usage, digital communities they're involved in, websites their visiting, malware programs installed, etc. As a diversity employer in the IT industry, we've found that discussions like these are often more complex than they seem at first.*

I also believe that people should be aware of what they are doing on their device and make sure that it is not affecting them in a negative way.

So, we started from just women, but till reaching the end we have covered several aspects that affect everyone, regardless of gender or age. And though we have covered a lot regarding this topic, there's a lot still left for the discussion.

HOW IS MY COUNTRY PERFORMING ON THE WEB? | INDIAN INTERNET

As many as 113 million users were affected by a form of online attacks in the past year, the India-specific report by Norton by Symantec said. On an average, an affected individual loses roughly Rs. 16,000 dealing with the fallout of cybercrimes, and as many as 30 hours in the aftermath of such an attack. "In the past year, 48 percent of India's online population or approximately 113 million Indians were affected by online crime," said Ritesh Chopra, Country Manager, India, Norton by Symantec.

Also, security levels in the country are so poor that around six million devices were estimated to have become 'slaves' to the Botnet attacks last year, said J. Satyanarayana, Advisor to the on Information Technology, Electronics and Communications and former Secretary to Government of India.

So, as the above news reports tell us, there is no other opinion that Indians has a very & great impact on the Internet & its population, but it still need a lot of improvement &

development in its several sectors including awareness & security of the Web.

Indian internet population- India has 45 million users on Facebook, 15 million on twitter and 45 million on LinkedIn from the total 125 million Internet users. (The amount is still growing.) And the 60% of social traffic comes from the non-metro cities of India. This shows us the wide range of Internet users in India and tells us that how important is Internet security for India, that Government should take seriously as a Big concern. Also, with the growth of Smartphones in today's world, the number of Internet users is greatly affected. There are more than 92+ Million active social media users that access accounts using their cell phones. This emerges the need of mobile safety & self-awareness about the Internet scams & scandals that are very popular & can be financially harmful in today's digital dependent world.

E-commerce- The Indian "online" advertising market has crossed Rs. 3000 cr. and the e-Commerce of India has crossed $24 billion (Rs 1,08,000 crores) which displays that increasing impact & influence of online market over the local markets, now the e-stores like Flipkart, Amazon, Snapdeal etc. are ruling the consumer's world, this e-market of India was $2.5 billion in 2009, it went up to $6.3b in 2011 & to $14b in 2012 and is still increasing along with the time. And according to Google India, there were 35 million online shoppers in India in 2014 which is expected to cross 100 million by 2017.

Kids on Social Networks- Do you know that on most of the social networking sites just allow people above 13 years of age to make an account? Yes, of course. But, according to a survey done by ASSOCHAM, about 73% of children from tier-

I & II cities between ages of 8 to 13 are using Facebook and other social networking sites. Sadly, in most cases, their elders/parents know about this & still they just don't care. However, many of them repent as their kids became addict to it. And it has many other bad effects along that including Cyber Bullying, online threat & immoral development.

And at the time of this survey's release, the Secretary-General of the organization, Mr. D S Rawat said, "*children are gaining access to social media sites at a younger age, which could expose them to content, people or situations that are out of their depth.*" So, what did he warned us about? If we check several other surveys, we will found that the majority of Cyber Bullying cases are about the children from the same age group (8 to 13). So, in a way the parents are leading children to a worse road of life.

As an Indian, I felt that I really needed to share this report with all my readers to help to understand that this whole thing is a very serious matter. And as the quote say, to clean the world we have to start from our own house.

THE INTERNET OF THE KIDS!

In today's world, everyone you know surfs The internet and more than half of the Internet's population consist of Teens & Kids and 72% of them are also active on social media. In this chapter, you will learn how the Internet works for the children and what they or their parents can do to make it safer for them.

KNOW WHAT THE INTERNET KNOWS ABOUT YOU!

Google your Name, email, blog, address & phone number to check your presence on the Internet. And to make it more effective, you can use some special websites that are made for this specified purpose:

www.zabasearch.com (Only for the US)

www.peekyou.com (World)

www.Google.com (Good old friend)

Other search engines (For full satisfaction)

Do remember that The internet is not a place where you can share or store your personal information including "private" pics, contacts & biodata, think of it as a public library where you don't want to store your private papers.

AND DON'T EVER REPEAT THESE THINGS:

I kept on telling people that they should not show, type or tell their passwords to anyone, even their closest friend. But, still people do that and end up crying, so stop doing that. And if you want to make your password more secure then head up to one of the previous chapters where I have shared some tips for doing that.

Also, 71% internet users access social media from their cell, so you can guess how important its security is. So make sure that you always password lock your phone and avoid storing your personal data on the device. And if you're engaged in mobile banking then you must have some backup security other than your bank's protection, for which I suggest any powerful antivirus. And avoid picking up calls or checking emails from unknown or untrusted people. And as your digital life is full of attackers, hackers & viruses so you need an antivirus to protect it. (Only if you can't protect yourself).This book also contains a chapter on that, if you have any confusion check it out.

ASPECIAL TOUR TO DEEP & DARK WEB!

Are you aware of the fact that you only **4%** of the Web is directly accessible and else is considered as "**Dark or Deep Web**" and the more important thing are that you can use that Deep web to browse the Internet hidden & free from all kind of trackers, hackers & advertisers! And before going deeper into the dark web, let's first learn some of its basics.

WHAT'S THE DIFFERENCE BETWEEN THE DARK WEB AND THE DEEP WEB? WHICH ARE WE TALKING ABOUT?

Dark Web or Deep Web or Deep net, Invisible Web, or Hidden Web, although all of these terms tend to be used interchangeably, they don't refer to exactly the same thing. The 'Deep Web' refers to all web pages that search engines cannot find. Thus the 'Deep Web' includes the 'Dark Web', but also includes all user databases, webmail pages & registration-required web forums. A basic thumb rule is that both, 'Dark Web' or 'Deep Web' are typically used by tabloid newspapers to refer to dangerous secret online worlds, the 'Dark Internet' is a boring place where scientists store raw data for research. The Deep Web is a catch-all term for all web pages that are not indexed for search. And here, we are basically talking about the deep web along talking a look at the vice world of Dark web.

Deep web, also known as the deep net is that portion of the internet whose content is not indexed by standard search engines and website. And early estimates suggest that the deep web is 4,000 to 5,000 times larger than the normal web. It means dark web covers up to **96%** of the internet.

HOW DOES IT REMAIN **HIDDEN**?

- Most of the content is intentionally hidden from the normal internet and is accessible only via special software.
- It contains some dynamic content which only response to a specified submitted query or accessed only through a form.
- It has the pages which are not linked to each other prevent that web programs (which are tended to access connected web page) from accessing the content.
- Some sites have password-protected resources.
- Some sites are limited to access their pages in only a technical way.

Coming to the uses, its potential is limitless:

- Many people use it for illegal or immoral purpose, but this thing can be very useful for private browsing.
- Even if your country doesn't provide you Right to Privacy, you can use this to work privately.

- In heavily censored countries, people use it to communicate and exchange information. And also to connect with the rest of the World.
- It prevents people from learning, tracking or using your location or personal data.
- It gives you access you to the information that "they" don't want you to know, like thousands of banned books, rumored alien documents, global

secrets and a lot of other sensitive & normal stuff.

Web based Hidden Services in January 2015[1]

Category	Percentage
Gambling	0.4
Guns	1.4
Chat	2.2
New (Not yet indexed)	2.2
Abuse	2.2
Books	2.5
Directory	2.5
Blog	2.75
Porn	2.75
Hosting	3.5
Hacking	4.25
Search	4.25
Anonymity	4.5
Forum	4.75
Counterfeit	5.2
Whistleblower	5.2
Wiki	5.2
Mail	5.7
Bitcoin	6.2
Fraud	9
Market	9
Drugs	15.4

(Image via Wikipedia, the free encyclopedia)

As you can see through the graph above, the Wikipedia reports that Dark web is mostly covered by the drugs & related services followed by market and of course fraud. Let's take a broader look at what it really had buried inside it:

- **Bitcoin services**: The only currency used here is Bitcoins making it a big market for the e-commerce sites. Also, for the illegal transactions & hacking services that provide & manipulate them.
- **Darknet markets:** From drugs to weapons, they sell everything that you can think of. Earlier last year, many of its commercial markets, which mediate transactions for illegal drugs and other goods, attracted significant media coverage starting with the popularity of Silk Road and its subsequent seizure by legal authorities.
- **Hacking services:** It feels like the most luxurious tool a computer hacker can get. This part of web allows a hackers to openly sell their services or as a part of groups. The best known till date are *Hackforum, Trojanforge, Mazafaka, darkode* and the *TheRealDeal darknet market*
- **Fraud services:** Here, you can get fraud credit cards, debit cards, bank accounts, phishing sites and anything you can imagine to use as a fraud tool.
- **Agent 47(s):** Yes! You read it right. Even though most of them are believed to be exclusively scams, there are reports that suggest powerful Hitmen activity. Even the creator of Silk Road was arrested by the FBI for his site and allegedly hiring a hitman to kill six people, although the charges. Along this urban legend, the story of Slender Man is also believed to be originated from here. And a creepy

game *Sad Satan* which was first reviewed by Youtubers Obscure Horror Corner which they claimed to have found via the dark web came to existence. And if you really want to know that, I have played it and it isn't any good that you may want to ever play.

- **Terrorism:** There are at least some real and fraudulent websites claiming to be used by *Daesh*, including a fake one seized in Operation *Onymous*.[42] In the wake of the November 2015 Paris attacks an actual such site was hacked by an *Anonymous* hacker group *GhostSec* and replaced with an advert for *Prozac*.

HOW CAN YOU ACCESS IT?

The most common used way is the access through special software such as **Tor**.

Some part of this web is also accessed by some custom hardware add-on(s) & proxy hacks that are used by only experts to access the deeper contents in Dark web. Leaving that part, for beginners, Go to ***www.torproject.org*** and download the Tor Browser Bundle, which contains all the required tools. Depending on what you intend to do on the Deep Web, there, reader, I leave you to your own devices and wish you good luck and safe surfing. And a warning before you goes any further.

Sites such as Reddit offer lists of links, as do several Wikis, including http://thehiddenwiki.org/ - a list that offers access to some very bad places. But I won't recommend going any deeper without any expert at your back. (I am serious!) And a basic tip: Dark Web sites do go down from time to time, due to their dark nature. But if you want good customer service, stay out of the dark!

NOW, SHOULD YOU ACCESS IT?

ISIS uses it. The Ashley Madison hackers used it. The Anonymous group did so. I won't recommend you to do what any of them did. This, "Heaven for Hackers" is a hell for the beginners. But, the user can remain anonymous using it if they play their cards right, which means they can exchange sensitive information without any major restriction. Coming to the point, the internet is made up of layers and just like the sea, as you will go deeper you will discover the undiscovered, but you will also need a lot of oxygen(safety in this case) at your back before you find the next Atlantis.

For now, just try to use it to protect your anonymity from unwanted trackers and leave your adventure skills for the day when you find your perfect guide. Most importantly, everyone should be aware of what is it and what impact it has on everyone's personal & professional life. And I did my part here.

Immune Web

MUCH OF IT MAY SEEM UNSAVORY,

BUT THE DARK WEB IS STILL
A POWERFUL TOOL

HARNESSED REGULARLY -- AND ONE
THAT CERTAINLY ISN'T GOING
ANYWHERE

UDAY VEER SINGH

WHAT I PERSONALLY LEARNT WHILE WRITING IMMUNE WEB?

About 2 and a half months ago, I started writing & learning about the Internet safety as a part of my personal goals and through it I have learnt that how important the security of this virtual world is; I saw & interviewed people, including my friends and many of them didn't even knew the basics of the Internet. It was a whole new thing for them. And this made me think and realize that the world I was living in; the people I was living with are utterly unaware of the virtual vices. Along with them, I have learnt many other things too that I want to share with you today:

Unawareness: As I said above, people are still unaware about the working and security of the web. Even after writing this I still feel that my readers are unaware of some topics that I have decided to surely cover in the future. Until then, make sure you follow my tips and don't let any crappy hacker attack you.

Carelessness: Whenever I question people about Internet safety, one of their popular answer is "Does it matter?" and eventually, my answer is Yes, but they just don't care about it. And this careless attitude is the major cause of the increasing cases of cyber crimes.

Women do have an Impact: Just like the real world, women have a great impact on the working of our virtual world. They are not minority or majority here, but they are the most popular target in cyber crimes. That will be so shameful for Tech geeks like me if we were unable to protect at least our friend girls, sister or girlfriends even in this small, but powerful world. But I have also realized that we will remain somehow unable to make any change unless a woman herself works in her uplifting; her self-education & awareness.

Some people can't make passwords: Sound hilarious, but maybe even your password isn't that secure. As we know, a password is a common 8 to 12 characters code that we use every day, but there are some specified rules that you need to follow for making it secure.

Bullying is more active than ever: Even today, Cyber-bullying is active but ignored topic that take place every day somewhere and people are unable to take action due to fear and sometimes even by their choice.

Fake accounts can be harmful even to the creator: They may seem harmless; people create them to irritate someone or just for random dating purpose, but if we look at its effect, we will found it as a very dangerous activity.

Our actions affect others seriously: We don't think that our words affect. (It was just a small comment, we think.) But in real, they do! And due to this; due to us, many beautiful souls die. This fact is sad but is still true and we should definitely take action about it!

The things that I have learned from while researching from Immune Web are limitless, but these were the brief of what I have learned from it. While the research, I also met & interviewed some people and I am very sorry not for sharing them all here, but below is some of the most interesting questions and most inspiring answers that I have collected from all of them:

Q. DO YOU FEEL SAFE WHILE USING THE WEB? DO YOU ALSO THINK THE SAME FOR YOUR MATE?

Maybe, I am somewhat same on the web, but for her my answer is No! The major reason behind this answer is that there are many what I call, cheap people around. All those unknown people on internet are the main cause, those who use it just to flirt & irritate others. They just look at a beautiful face and start sending bad messages to her.

Q. CAN WE MAKE IT BETTER?

Maybe, yes, but I am not sure about that. Some basic precautions can be taken like girls should not accept the friend request of people who are unknown to her and if they message they should not reply, she must known the surrounding of her area and her profile must be within her friends not so in the public.

Reply: Basically, for this answer, I am utterly against you. Can't we make this world safe enough that someone can do what she wanted to? Why do the girls have to always follow some guidelines? Why can't we make those 'cheap' people who are a blemish on the name of all men realize their mistakes? Some common precautions are acceptable, but limiting someone to an area, just because the world is full of jerks; this in unacceptable; utterly annul!

Q. WHAT ARE YOUR VIEWS ABOUT PRIVACY?

Privacy doesn't matter friends, but it does in the public. It's on someone's thinking if he/she likes to share his/her privacy with anyone.

Q. WHAT DOES A SAFE INTERNET LOOKS LIKE TO YOU?

The security must be the first thing in the list of developments. I want the Internet to be developed like if someone sends me a bad photo, he must be spam within no time. And coming to government, it can only employ some smart tech guys like you that can web secure, at least in their area. Immune Web in every locality where people come and discuss the internet and its security flaws than there will be no need of antiviruses, security specialists, and girls' worries. But until that day, this guide will keep you safe at a fine level.

THANK

YOU!

WHAT ELSE DO WE DO?

THEORY OF MANKIND is a project started to inspire & present people by Ideas that they have never thought, by Concepts they have never heard and by Mysteries they have never researched. From Humanity to the Politics, it will cover the widest range of unique and common subjects, and with every new topic, you will see vision widening, new doors opening and new Ideas developing.

HOW IS IT DIFFERENT?

There are many scientific or philosophical blog out there, but ToM is different from them:

- No other blog will teach & inspire you about Humanity, Science & Philosophy all at one place like us.
- All of our work is based on our real experiments, researches, and studies. We check & experiment every Idea and concept before presenting it to our audience.
- We are creating a team of different people, all from a unique field of study, but with a single aim of development of Humanity.